I ♥ gratitude

vol. III

I ♥ gratitude

my first gratitude journal

Did you know?
(fun facts)

VOL. III

MICHELLE LEE-KING
MYA HARPER KING

Harper Girl Press, LLC

I Heart Gratitude, Did You Know? vol. III
May 2018
Copyright © 2018 by Michelle Lee-King and Mya Harper King. All rights reserved.

Published by Harper Girl Press, LLC
www.harpergirlpress.com

Book design copyright © 2017 by Harper Girl Press LLC. All rights reserved.
Cover design by Michelle Lee-King
Interior design by Michelle Lee-King

Published in the United States of America

ISBN:978-0-692-07731-3

Dedicated To: You

Be amazing

Be good

Be smart

Be cool

Be yourself

This is me

```
┌─────────────────────────┐
│                         │
│                         │
│                         │
│       PLACE             │
│     PHOTO HERE          │
│                         │
│                         │
│                         │
└─────────────────────────┘
```

This journal belongs to: _____

I started this journal on: _____

I am _____ years old.

My favorite food is _____.

My favorite TV show is_____.

I am going to change the world by_____.

Parents,

This world can be a crazy environment for a young mind.
(And sometimes older minds, too!)

It can seem like we're surrounded by negative energy, circumstances
that are less than ideal and trying times.

The best part?

There's a simple change you can implement — today — with your
children to help shape their world into a positive one.

How? Through 60 days of inspired, fun, creative prompts!

**We can live in a world where our kids experience positivity,
hope, and thankfulness.**

We can teach our kids to be genuinely grateful for what they have, and
aware that there's more to life than always getting what they want.

We can live in a brighter world where our kids learn to be thoughtful,
grateful   human beings long before they hit their teenage years (and
won't that make those teenage years easier to handle!).

My message is simple: grateful children=happy children.

We adults already know how powerful gratitude can be.
It's time to pass that power on to our kids.

When we feel empowered through gratitude, our whole world can
change.

- Parenting becomes smoother.
- Relationships become stronger.
- Children become happier.

And all it takes is 60 days of gratitude.

Beautiful Young Person,

I am excited to know that you have this journal in your hands.
You are about to start an exciting journey into the world of gratitude.

What is Gratitude?

Gratitude is the quality of being thankful. It involves
recognizing and appreciating the "good things" that already
exist in your life.

What to Be Grateful For?

You can be grateful for places, such as your home. You can be
grateful for people, such as your parents or friends. Physical
possessions, like your favorite toy, your TV or computer. Also,
be grateful for intangibles such as a fun experience, your
freedom, love and friendship.

What's the Big Deal about Gratitude?

Gratitude is truly a choice. You can choose to be grateful or
you can choose not to be. It's that simple! By writing in this journal
you are making the choice to focus on what makes you happy.

Gratitude is important because what you focus on grows. If
you focus all your energy on the things you are grateful for,
you will attract more things into your life to be grateful for.

focus on the good
more good comes your way

How to use this gratitude journal:

- Keep this journal near your bed.

- Write the date.

- Write three things you are grateful for and discuss why (This might be something that happened to you today, something a friend did for you, something you have or something you did for someone else). Do not repeat the previous day's entries. **You must list three new items each day (no repeats).**

- Have fun reading the "did you know" facts.

- Repeat daily!

Example: Today I am grateful for...

1. A sunny day
2. My parents
3. Having enough food to eat

Start practicing gratitude!

HAPPINESS ISN'T ABOUT GETTING WHAT YOU WANT ALL THE TIME.

IT'S ABOUT LOVING WHAT YOU HAVE AND BEING GRATFEUL FOR IT.

-UNKNOWN

Date:

Today I am grateful for...

1. _____

2. _____

3. _____

Did you know?

It is impossible for most people to lick their own elbow (try it!).

(see if you are one of the few who can)

Date:

Today I am grateful for...

1. _____

2. _____

3. _____

Did you know?

A crocodile cannot stick it's tongue out.

Date:

Today I am grateful for...

1. _____

2. _____

3. _____

Did you know?

The dot on top of the letter 'i' and 'j' is called a tittle.

Date:

Today I am grateful for...

1. _____

2. _____

3. _____

Did you know?

Kangaroos cannot walk backwards.

Date:

Today I am grateful for...

1. _____

2. _____

3. _____

Did you know?

Cat urine glows under
a black light.

Date:

Today I am grateful for...

1. _____

2. _____

3. _____

Did you know?

Like fingerprints, everyone's tongue print is different.

Date:

Today I am grateful for...

1. _____

2. _____

3. _____

Did you know?

A shark is the only known fish that can blink with both eyes.

Date:

Today I am grateful for...

1. _____

2. _____

3. _____

Did you know?

*Maine is the only state
that has a one syllable name.*

Date:

Today I am grateful for...

1. _____

2. _____

3. _____

Did you know?

A cat has 32 muscles in each ear.

Date:

Today I am grateful for...

1. _____

2. _____

3. _____

Did you know?

An ostrich's eye is bigger than it's brain.

Date:

Today I am grateful for...

1. _____

2. _____

3. _____

Did you know?

Tigers have stripped skin, not just stripped fur.

Date:

Today I am grateful for...

1. _____

2. _____

3. _____

Did you know?

A dime has 118 ridges around the edge.

Date:

Today I am grateful for...

1. _____

2._____

3._____

Did you know?

The giant squid has the largest eyes in the world.

Date:

Today I am grateful for...

1. _____

2. _____

3. _____

Did you know?

Your thigh bone is stronger than concrete.

Date:

Today I am grateful for...

1. _____

2. _____

3. _____

Did you know?

A sneeze travels at over
100 miles per hour.

Date:

Today I am grateful for...

1. _____

2. _____

3. _____

Did you know?

We cut down around 27,000 trees every day to make toilet paper.

Date:

Today I am grateful for...

1. _____

2. _____

3. _____

Did you know?

An apple is 25% air, that is why it floats on water.

Date:

Today I am grateful for...

1. _____

2. _____

3. _____

Did you know?

70% of the Earth's surface is covered in water.

Date:

Today I am grateful for...

1. _____

2. _____

3. _____

Did you know?

Octopuses have three hearts.

Date:

Today I am grateful for...

1. _____

2. _____

3. _____

Did you know?

Grasshoppers spit at their enemies.

Date:

Today I am grateful for...

1. _____

2. _____

3. _____

Did you know?

Bats can eat about 3000 bugs in a night.

Date:

Today I am grateful for...

1. _____

2. _____

3. _____

Did you know?

The oldest living tree in the world is in California, and is around 4,847 years old.

Date:

Today I am grateful for...

1. _____

2. _____

3. _____

Did you know?

Goats' have rectangular pupils.

Date:

Today I am grateful for...

1. _____

2. _____

3. _____

Did you know?

The lines in the sky made by airplanes are called contrails.

Date:

Today I am grateful for...

1. _____

2. _____

3. _____

Did you know?

An elephant's skin is so
sensitive that it can feel
a fly landing on it.

Date:

Today I am grateful for...

1. _____

2. _____

3. _____

Did you know?

Zimbabwe's first President was President Banana.

Date:

Today I am grateful for...

1. _____

2. _____

3. _____

Did you know?

There is a type of frog that hears through its mouth.

Date:

Today I am grateful for...

1. _____

2. _____

3. _____

Did you know?

Some butterflies drink tears of turtles.

Date:

Today I am grateful for...

1. _____

2. _____

3. _____

Did you know?

There is a professional
Rock Paper Scissor league.

Date:

Today I am grateful for...

1. _____

2. _____

3. _____

Did you know?

A chameleon's tongue is more than double the length of it's body.

Date:

Today I am grateful for...

1. _____

2. _____

3. _____

Did you know?

There is a city in Turkey called Batman.

Date:

Today I am grateful for...

1. _____

2. _____

3. _____

Did you know?

There is a town in Denmark called Middelfart.

Date:

Today I am grateful for...

1. _____

2. _____

3. _____

Did you know?

For 20 years, the mayor of Talkeetna, Alaska was a cat.

Date:

Today I am grateful for...

1. _____

2. _____

3. _____

Did you know?

When threatened, sea cucumbers sometimes shoot their internal organs out of their butts.

Date:

Today I am grateful for...

1. _____

2. _____

3. _____

Did you know?

Human ears and noses never stop growing.

Date:

Today I am grateful for...

1. _____

2. _____

3. _____

Did you know?

"Eructation" is the scientific

word for burping.

Date:

Today I am grateful for...

1. _____

2. _____

3. _____

Did you know?

There are 24 known species of dancing frogs.

Date:

Today I am grateful for...

1. _____

2. _____

3. _____

Did you know?

In 2007, worms fell from the sky in a town in Louisiana.

Date:

Today I am grateful for...

1. _____

2. _____

3. _____

Did you know?

Reindeer eyes turn blue

in the Winter.

Date:

Today I am grateful for...

1. _____

2. _____

3. _____

Did you know?

A bee has five eyes.

Date:

Today I am grateful for...

1. _____

2. _____

3. _____

Did you know?

There is a town in Colorado called No Name.

Date:

Today I am grateful for...

1. _____

2. _____

3. _____

Did you know?

There is a type of cheese that is purposely filled with bugs.

Date:

Today I am grateful for...

1. _____

2. _____

3. _____

Did you know?

In Japan, Ronald McDonald
is called Donald McDonald.

Date:

Today I am grateful for...

1. _____

2. _____

3. _____

Did you know?

Most bears have 42 teeth.

Date:

Today I am grateful for...

1. _____

2. _____

3. _____

Did you know?

M&M's chocolate stands for the initials for its inventors Mars and Murrie.

Date:

Today I am grateful for...

1. _____

2. _____

3. _____

Did you know?

There is a town called Why, Arizona and another named Why Not, Mississippi.

Date:

Today I am grateful for...

1. _____

2. _____

3. _____

Did you know?

Honey is the only natural food that does not spoil.

Date:

Today I am grateful for...

1. _____

2. _____

3. _____

Did you know?

The only animal that runs faster that an ostrich is a cheetah.

Date:

Today I am grateful for...

1. _____

2. _____

3. _____

Did you know?

Fleas can jump higher than 100 times their height.

Date:

Today I am grateful for...

1. _____

2. _____

3. _____

Did you know?

Monkeys can go bald in old age, just like humans.

Date:

Today I am grateful for...

1. _____

2. _____

3. _____

Did you know?

Frogs don't drink; they absorb water through their skin.

Date:

Today I am grateful for...

1. _____

2. _____

3. _____

Did you know?

A group of frogs is called an army.

Date:

Today I am grateful for...

1. _____

2. _____

3. _____

Did you know?

A cloud can weigh more than
a million pounds.

Date:

Today I am grateful for...

1. _____

2. _____

3. _____

Did you know?

Starfish do not have brains.

Date:

Today I am grateful for...

1. _____

2. _____

3. _____

Did you know?

A peanut is not a nut.

Date:

Today I am grateful for...

1. _____

2. _____

3. _____

Did you know?

Hummingbirds are the only birds that can fly backwards.

Date:

Today I am grateful for...

1. _____

2. _____

3. _____

Did you know?

A Zedonk is a cross between zebra and a donkey.

Date:

Today I am grateful for...

1. _____

2. _____

3. _____

Did you know?

There is a lake in Australia that is completely pink.

Date:

Today I am grateful for...

1. _____

2. _____

3. _____

Did you know?

A giraffe cleans its ears with its 21-inch tongue.

Date:

Today I am grateful for...

1. _____

2. _____

3. _____

Did you know?

Dragonflies sometimes eat each other.

Date:

Today I am grateful for...

1. _____

2. _____

3. _____

Did you know?

A lightning bold is 5x hotter than the sun.

Congratulations on completing your 60 days of gratitude.

You are now officially a "Gratitude Superhero."

How cool is that?

There is a lot of responsibility that goes along with being a "Gratitude Superhero." As a Superhero, you are more appreciative, considerate, loving, and always thinking of ways to give back to the world.

Always remember that in life sometimes you get what you want, sometimes you get what you need and sometimes you just get what you get. Be grateful for it all.

Complete the promise card on the next page to activate your gratitude superpowers and start sharing your goodness with the world.

Have fun!

I,_____, promise to give without expecting and bring joy to my neighbors by lending a helping hand.

Think about the positive!

Perform Random Acts of Kindness and give back to the world. ✔

PURSUE MY DREAMS

DO MY PART TO CHANGE THE WORLD AROUND ME

Choose gratitude & love over entitlement and negativity.

Be a ray of sunshine with a generous spirit.

Ask, "what's good about this?" in every situation

I WILL BE GRATEFUL.

www.iheartgratitude.com

73

Did You Know References:

Pg. 12 – www.bbc.com
Pg. 13 – www.dictionary.com
Pg. 14 – www.ipfactly.com
Pg. 15 - www.thoughtco.com
Pg. 16 – www.thestar.com
Pg. 17 - www.reference.com
Pg. 18 – www.wisegeek.com
Pg. 19 – www.catsinternational.org
Pg. 20 – www.softschools.com
Pg. 21 – www.nationalgeographic.com
Pg. 22 – www.history.com
Pg. 23 – www.nationalgeographic.com
Pg. 24 – www.livescience.com
Pg. 25 – www.lung.org
Pg. 26 – www.nationalgeographic.org
Pg. 27 – www.producepedia.com
Pg. 28 - www.universetoday.com
Pg. 29 – www.sciencefocus.com
Pg. 30 – www.thoughtco.com
Pg. 31 – www.bugrunner.com
Pg. 32 – www.livescience.com
Pg. 33 – www.science20.com
Pg. 34 – www.dictionary.com
Pg. 35 – www.cbsnews.com
Pg. 36 – www.ifps.io
Pg. 37 – www.livescience.com
Pg. 38 – www.nationalgeographic.com
Pg. 39 – www.worldrps.com
Pg. 40 – www.nationalgeographic.com
Pg. 41 – www.britannica.com
Pg. 42 – www.middelfart.dk
Pg. 43 – www.google.com
Pg. 44 – www.nationalgeographic.com
Pg. 45 – www.doctoroz.com
Pg.46 – www.dictionary.com
Pg. 47 - www.nationalgeographic.com

Did You Know References:

Pg. 48 – www.wafb.com

Pg. 49 – www.livescience.com

Pg. 50 - www.sweetreehoney.com

Pg. 51 – www.suburbanstats.org

Pg. 52 – www.seriouseats.com

Pg. 53 – www.kotaku.com

Pg. 54 – www.bear.org

Pg. 55 – www.businessinsider.com

Pg. 56 – www.whynotnowms.org

Pg. 56 – www.arizona-demographics.com

Pg. 57 – www.smithsonianmag.com

Pg. 58 – www.safariostrich.co.za

Pg. 59 – www.pesthack.com

Pg. 60 – www.animalanswers.co.uk

Pg. 61 – www.burkemuseum.org

Pg. 62 – www.allaboutfrogs.org

Pg. 63 – www.sciencealert.com

Pg. 64 – www.whalefacts.org

Pg. 65 – www.peanut-institute.org

Pg. 66 – www.ponderweasel.com

Pg. 67 – www.animals.net

Pg. 68 – www.australiangeographic.com

Pg. 69 – www.listverse.com

Pg. 70 – www.dragonflywebsite.com

Pg. 71 – www.seeker.com